ALPHABET

BIG

LATTER

A =

APPLE

B = 🏐

BALL

B B B B

B B B B

B B B B

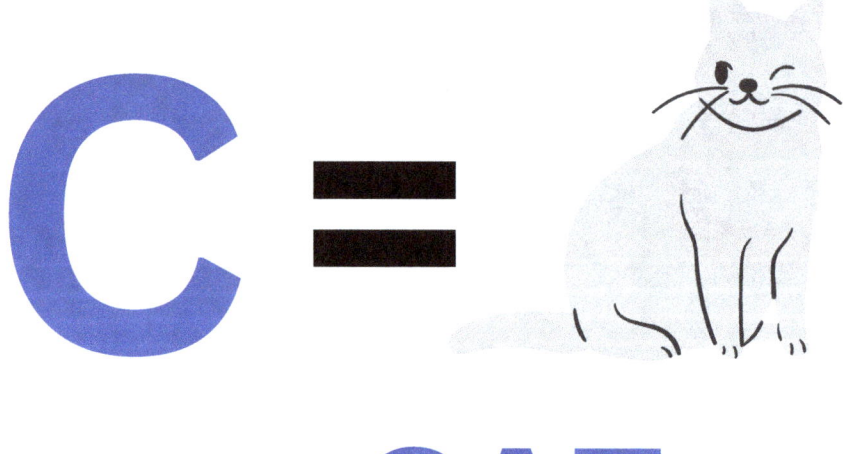

C =

CAT

D = 🐕

DOG

D D D D

D D D D

D D D D

E =

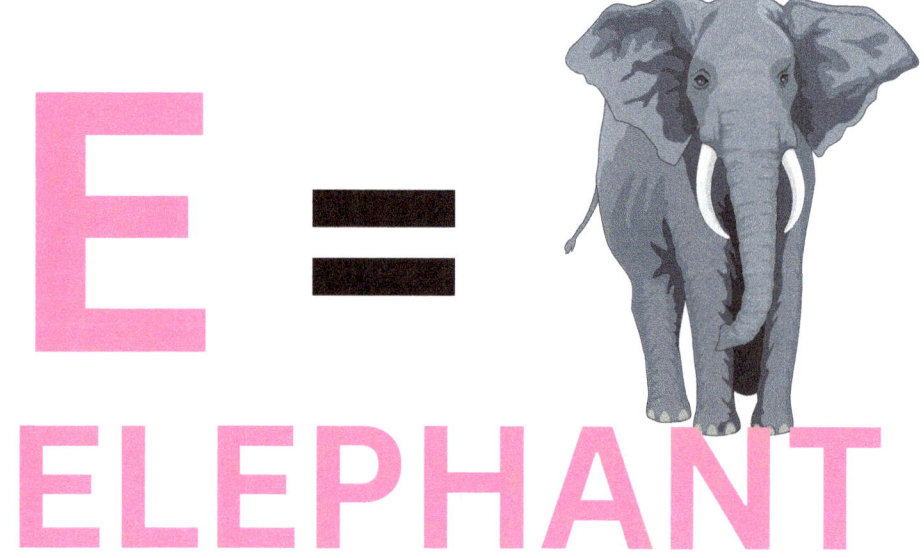

ELEPHANT

F = FISH

F F F F

F F F F

F F F F

G = 🐐

GOAT

H = 🎩

HAT

H H H H

H H H H

H H H H

I =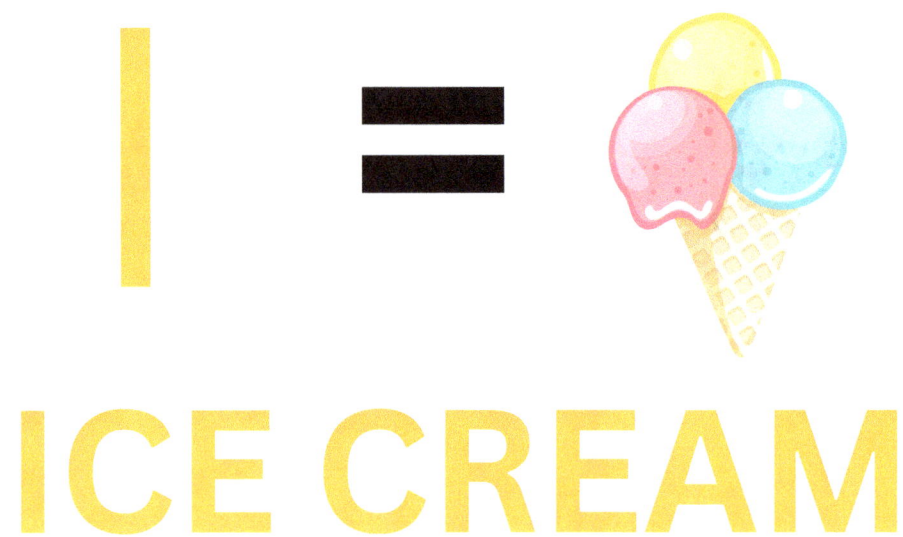

ICE CREAM

J =

JUG

K =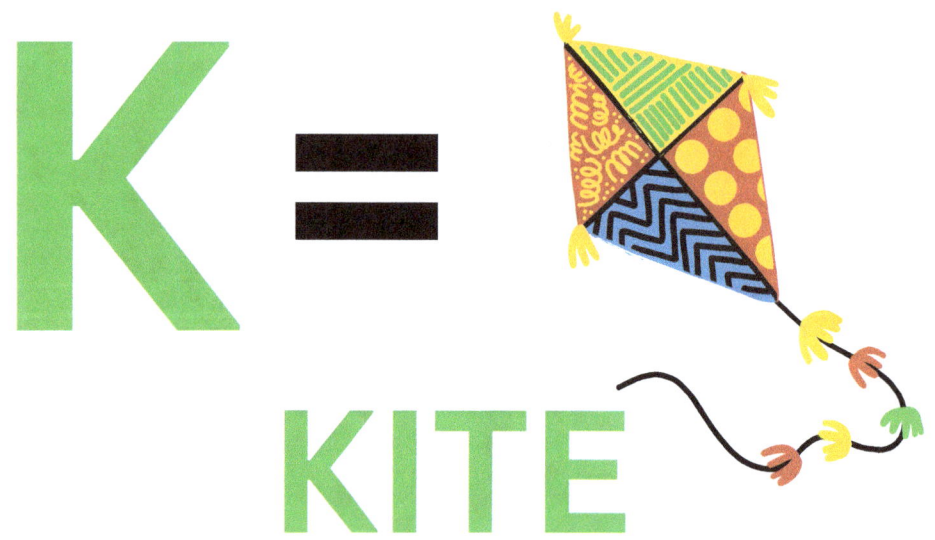

KITE

L =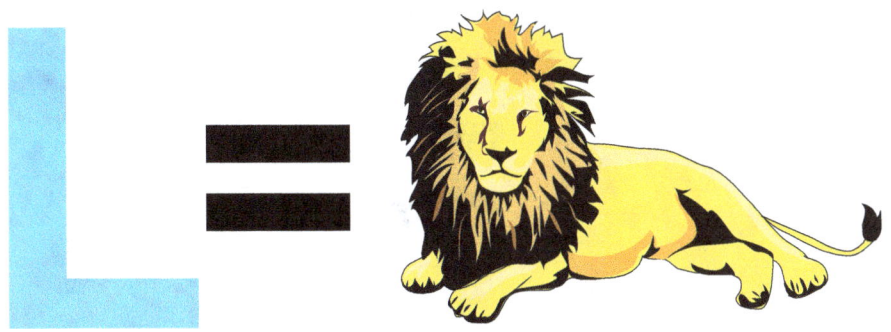

LION

M =

MONKEY

N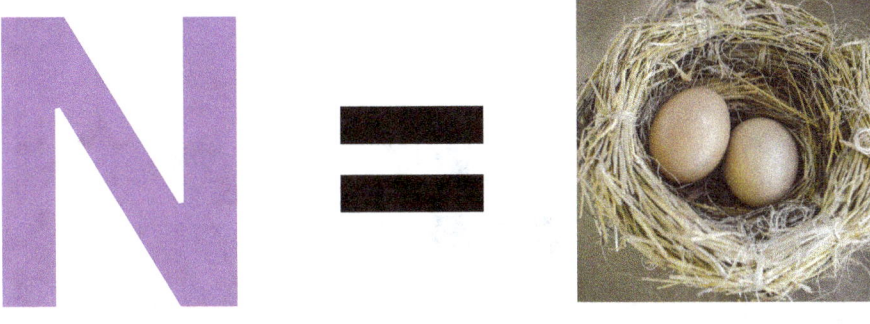

NEST

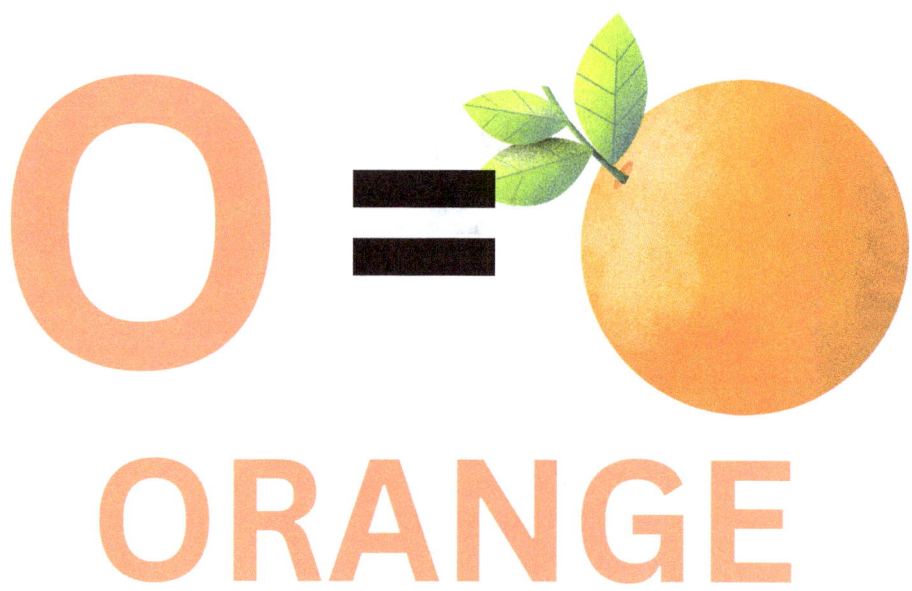

ORANGE

P =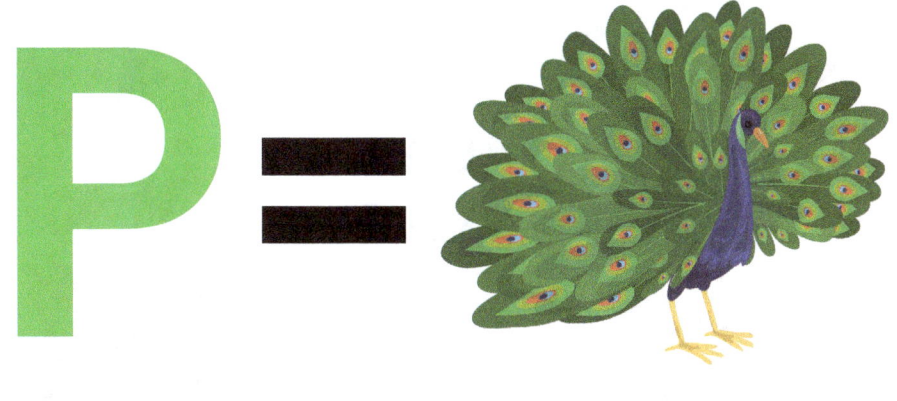

PEACOCK

Q =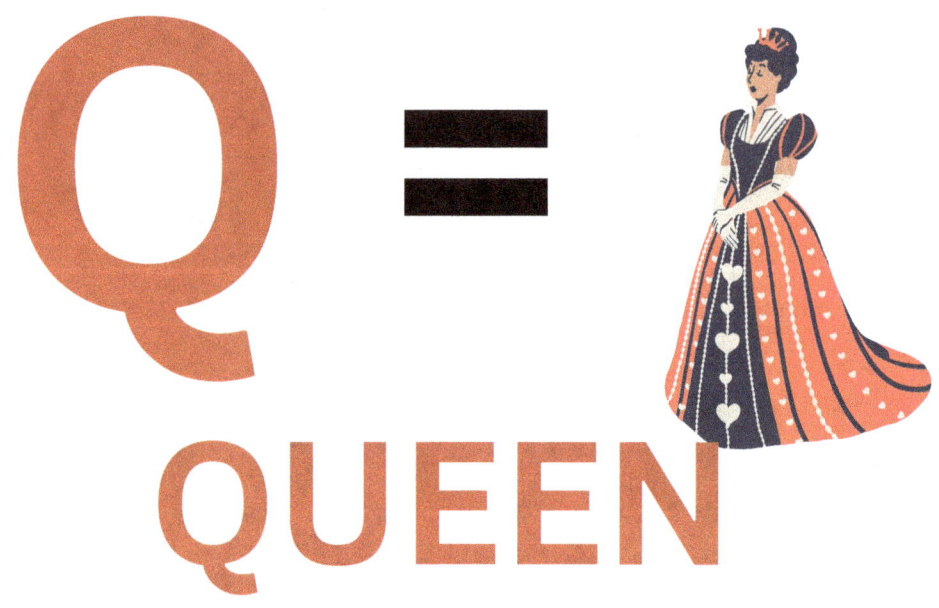

QUEEN

R = RABBIT

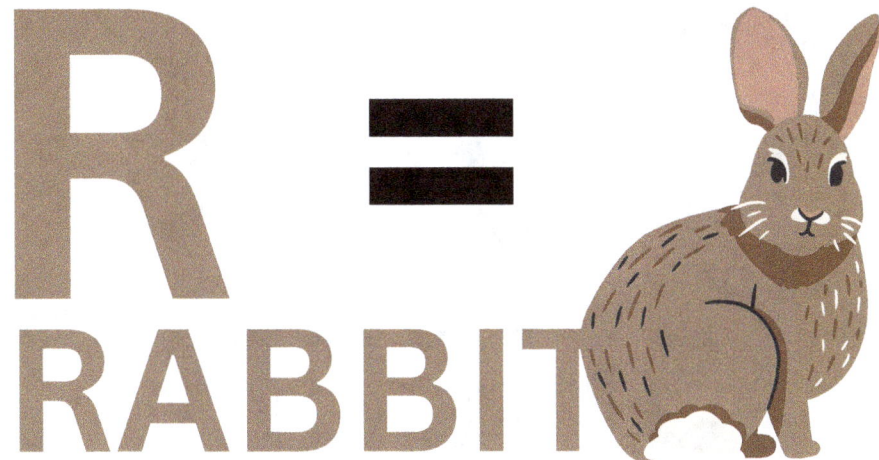

R R R R

R R R R

R R R R

S = 🐑

SHEEP

T =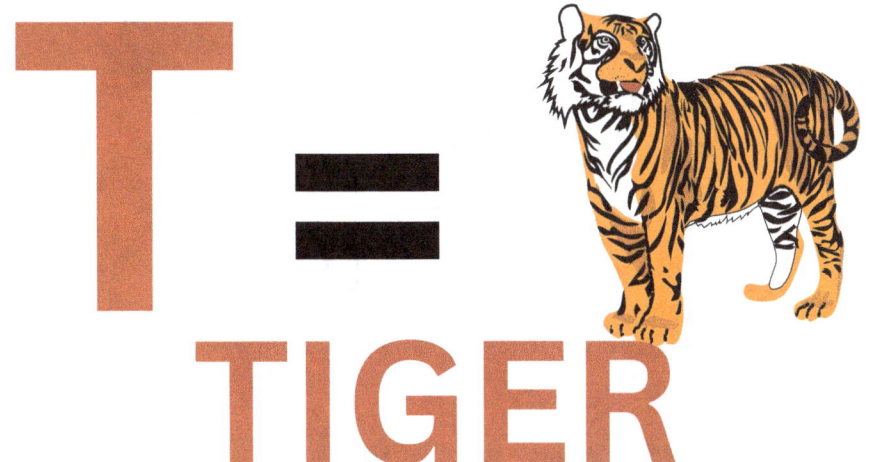

TIGER

U =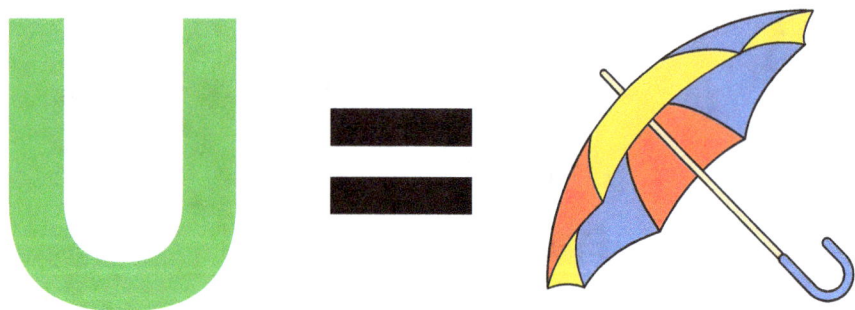

UMBRELLA

V =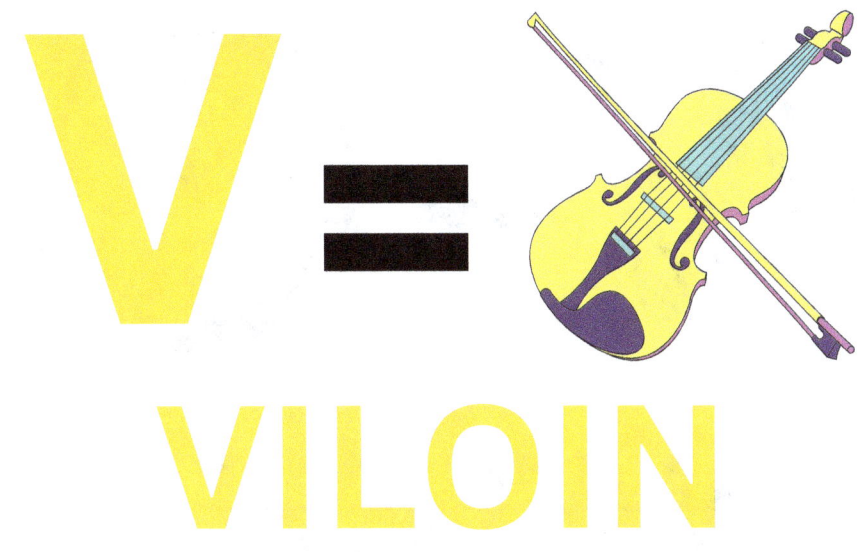

VILOIN

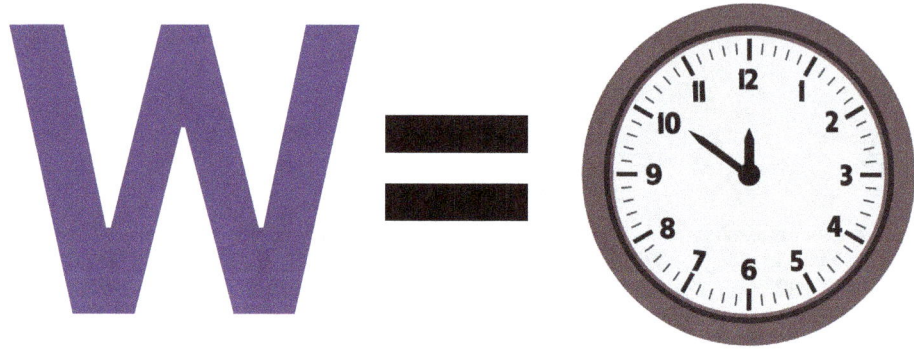

WATCH

X =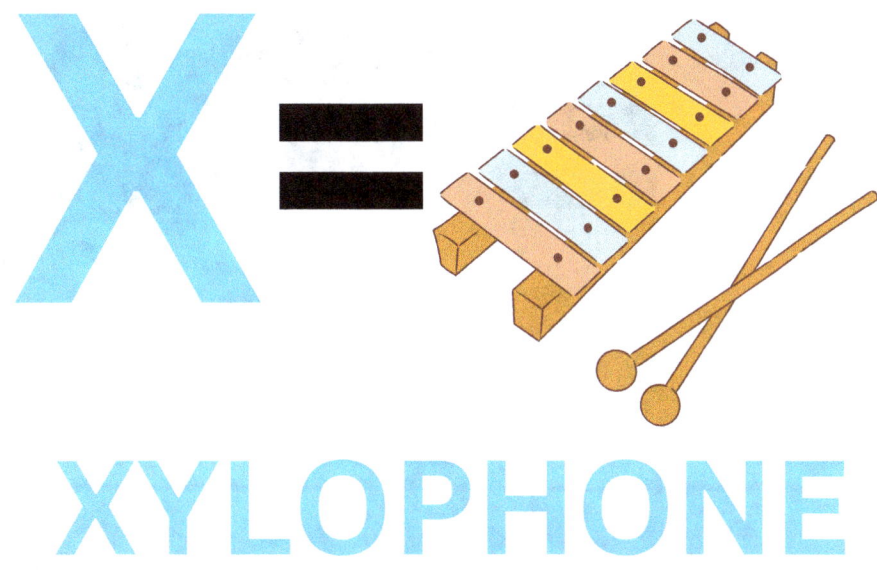

XYLOPHONE

Y=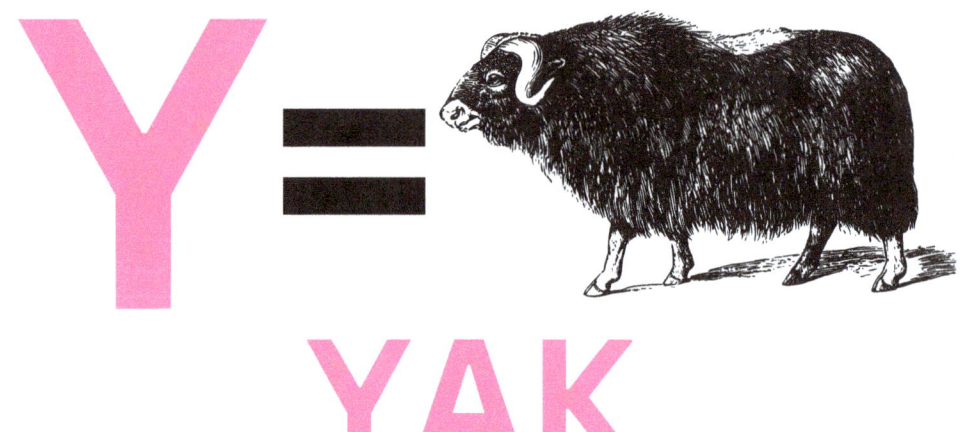

YAK

Z =

ZEBRA

ALPHABET
SMALL
LATTER

a

a a a a a

a a a a

a a a a

b

b b b b

b b b b

b b b b

C

C C C C

C C C C

C C C C

d

d d d d

d d d d

d d d d

e

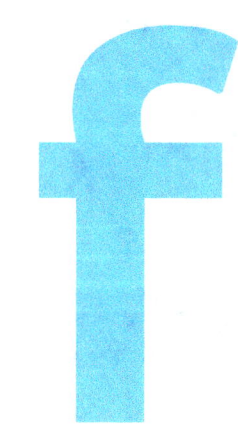

g

g g g g

g g g g

g g g g

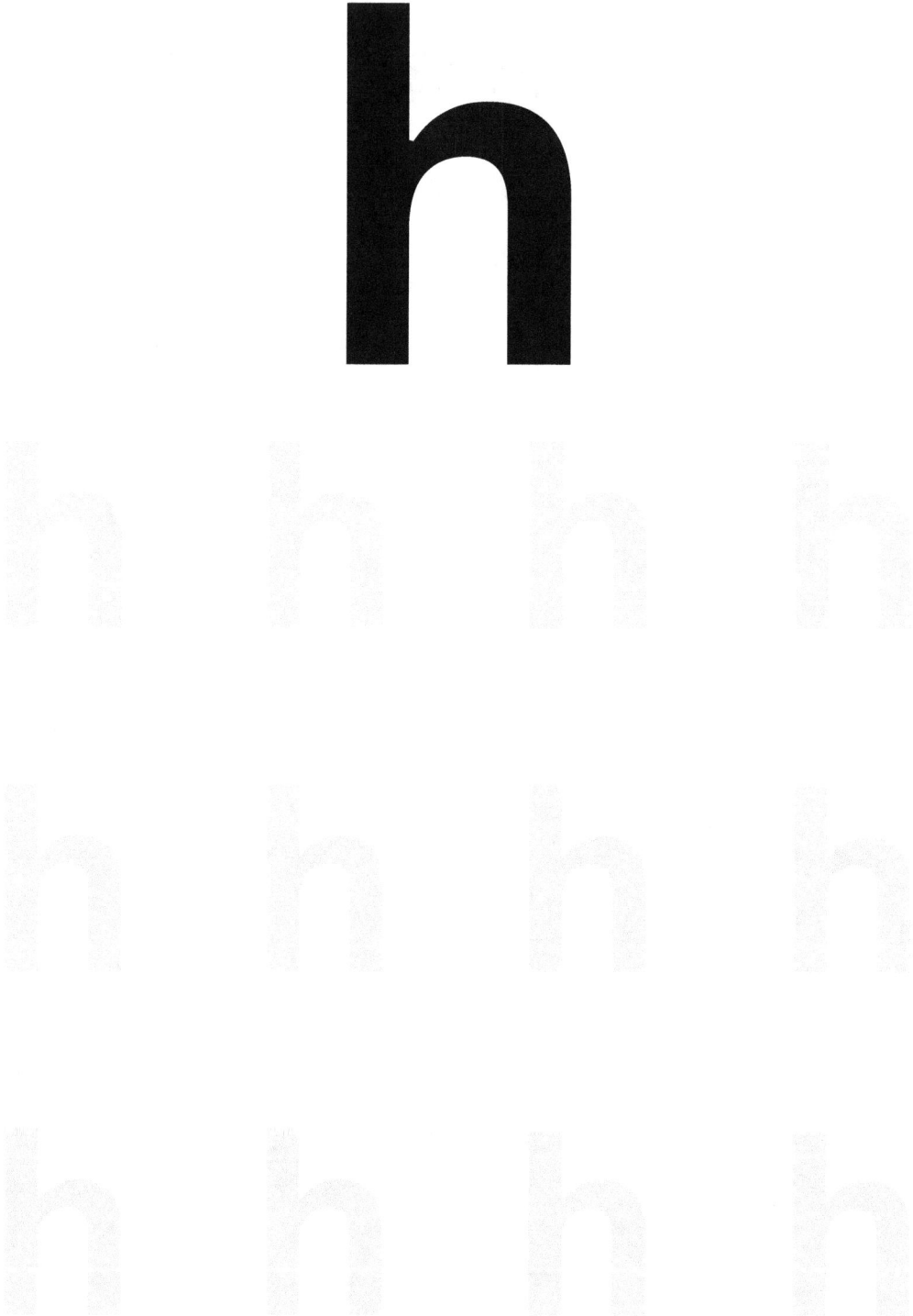

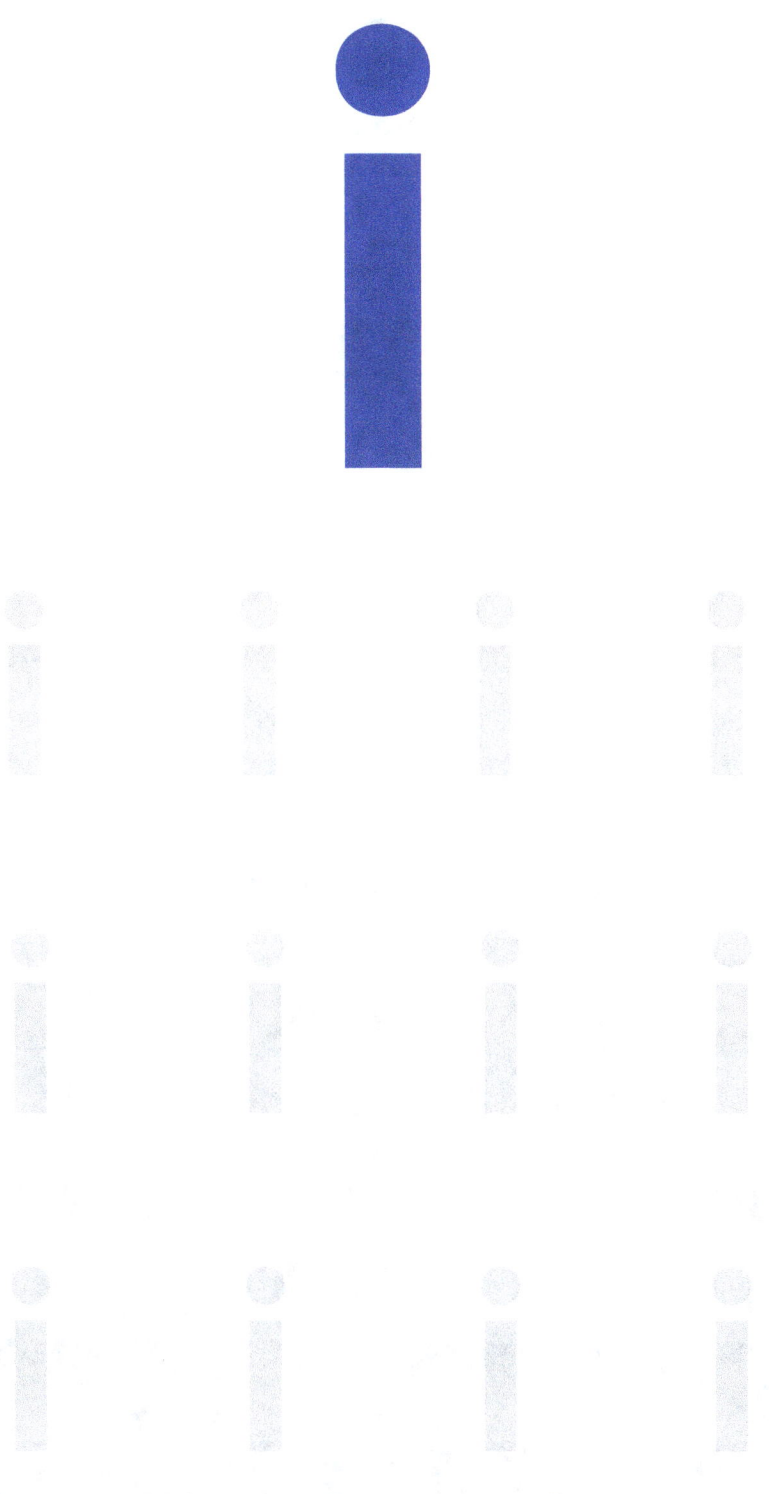

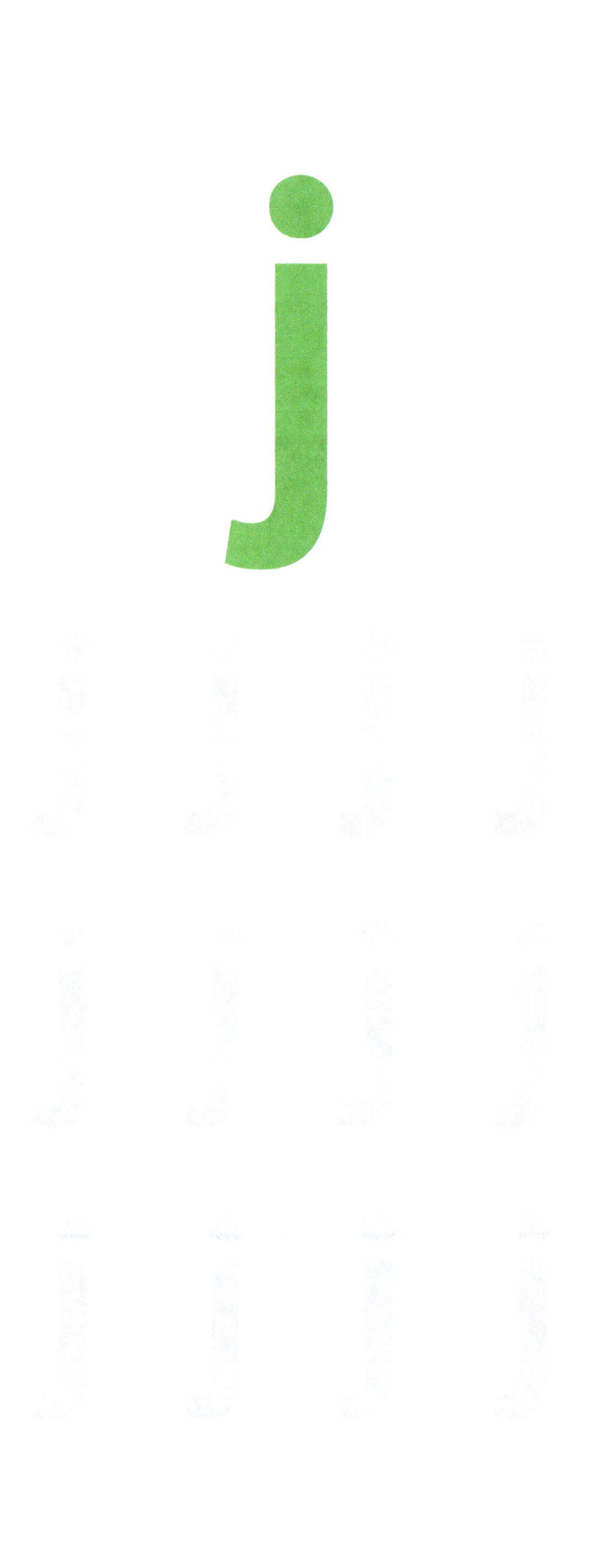

k

k k k k

k k k k

k k k k

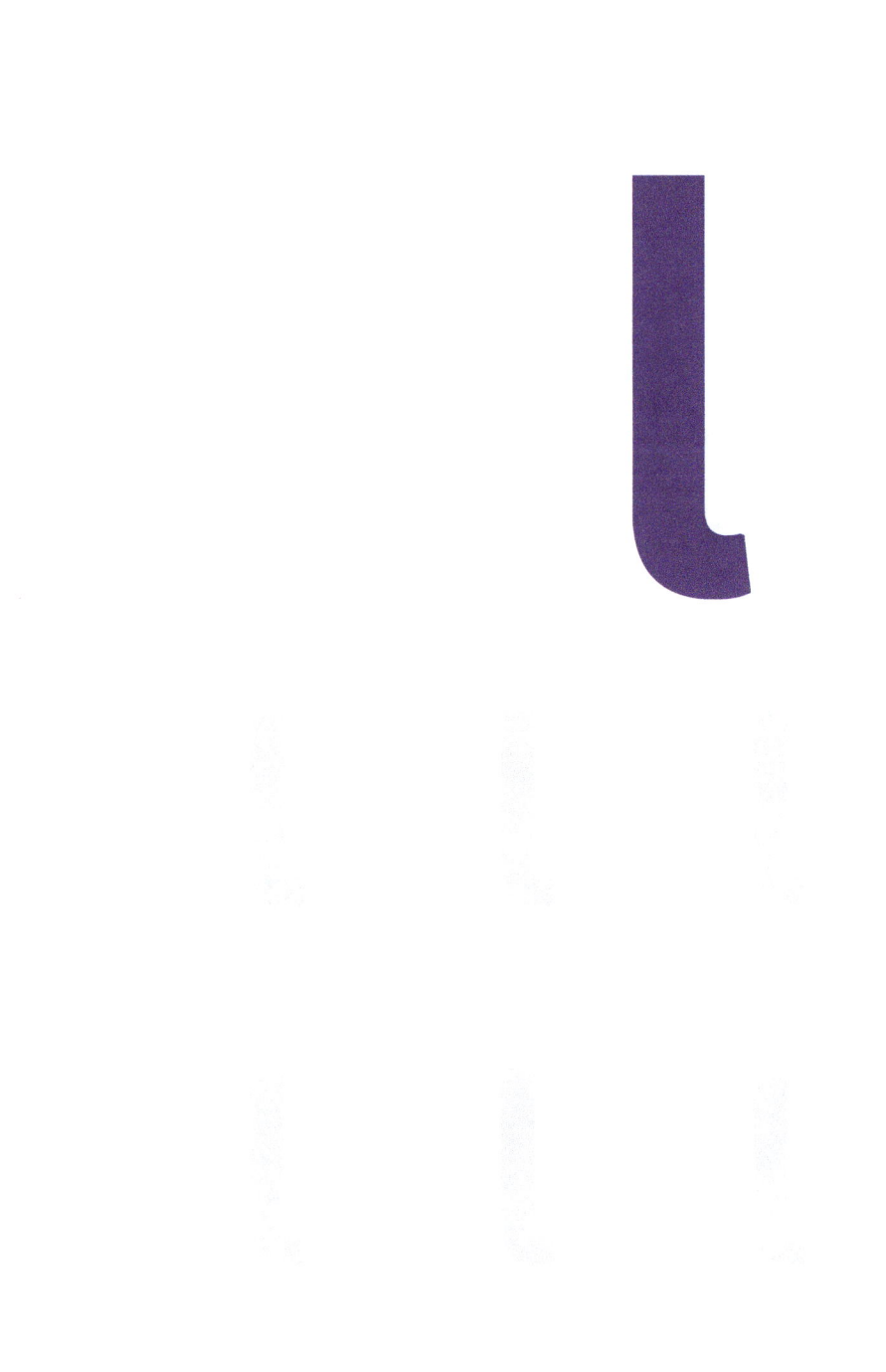

m

m m m m

m m m m

m m m m

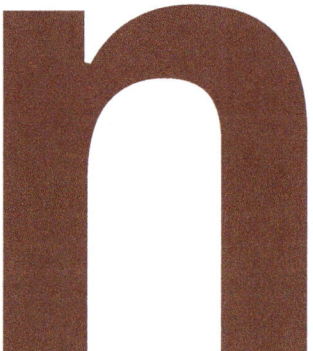

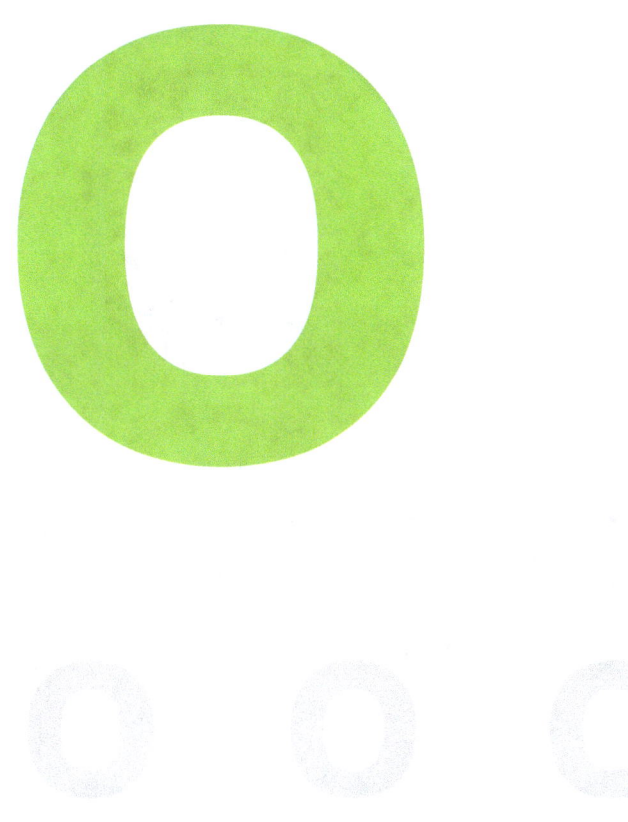

p

q

q q q q

q q q q

q q q q

S

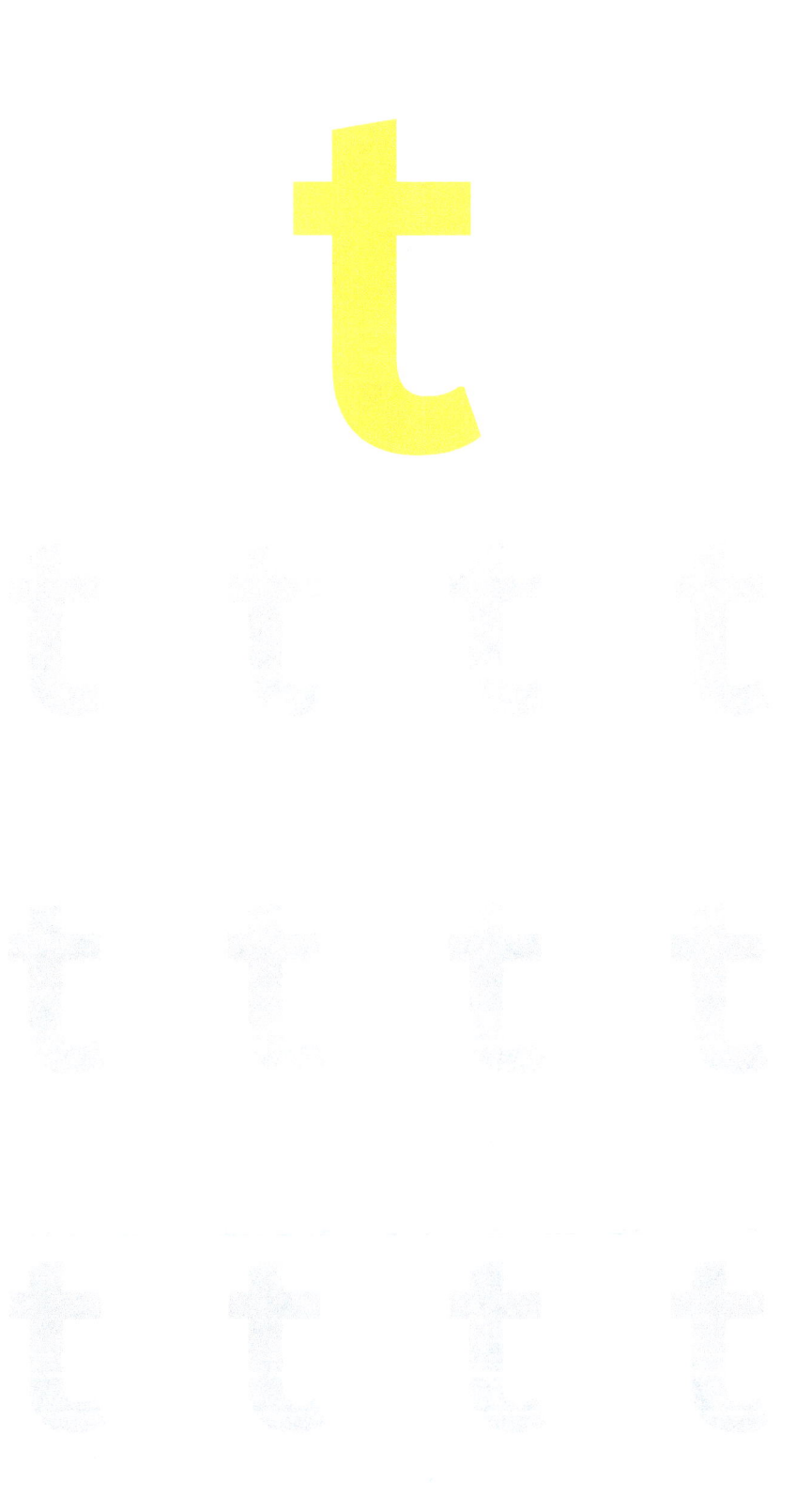

u

u u u u

u u u u

u u u u

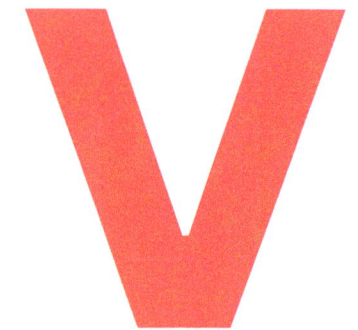

W

W W W W

W W W W

W W W W

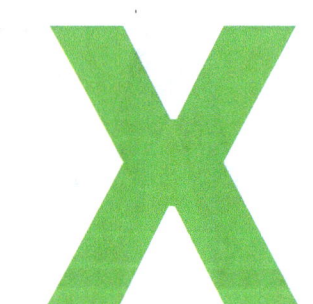

y

y y y y

y y y y

y y y y

z

COLORING
PAGES

A

APPLE

B

BALL

C

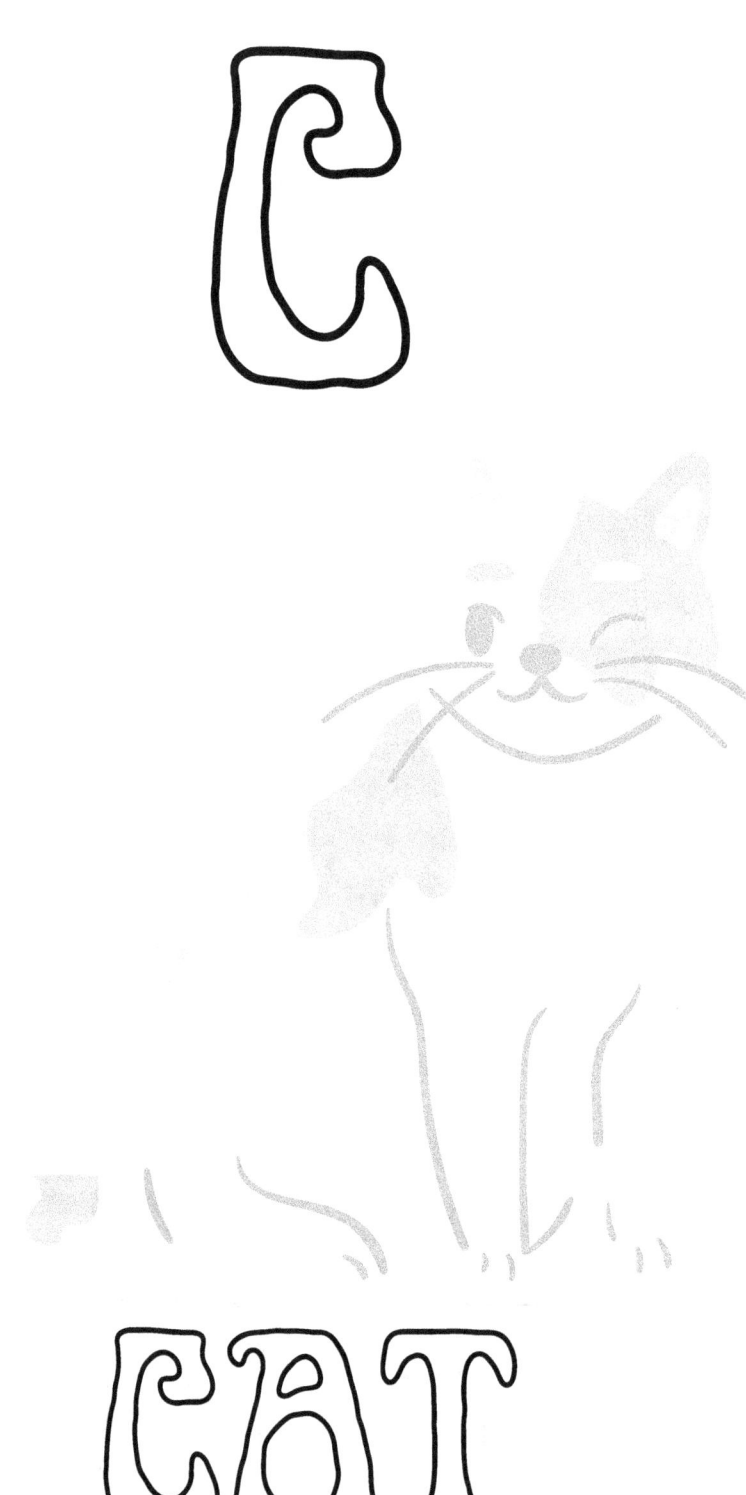

CAT

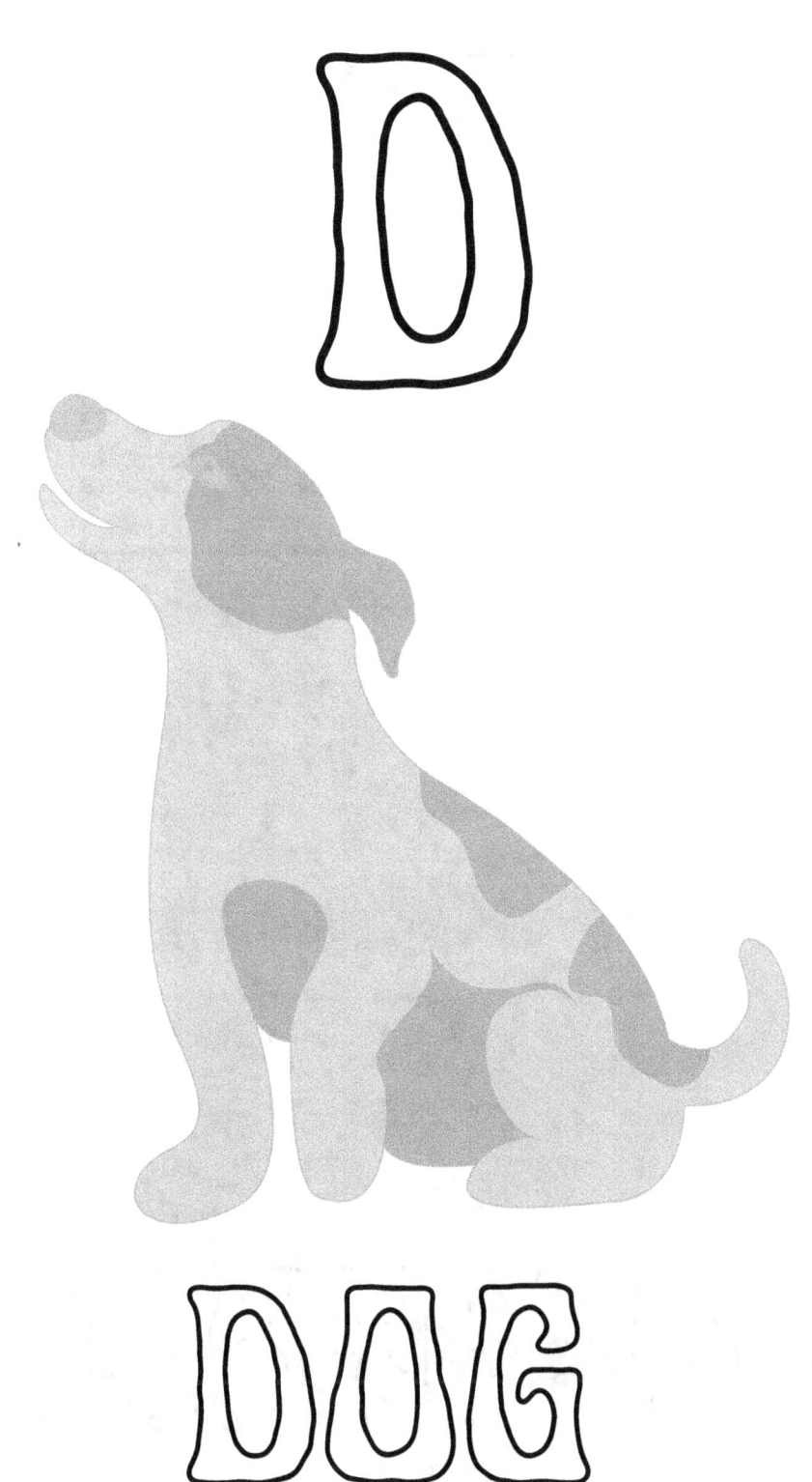

D

DOG

E

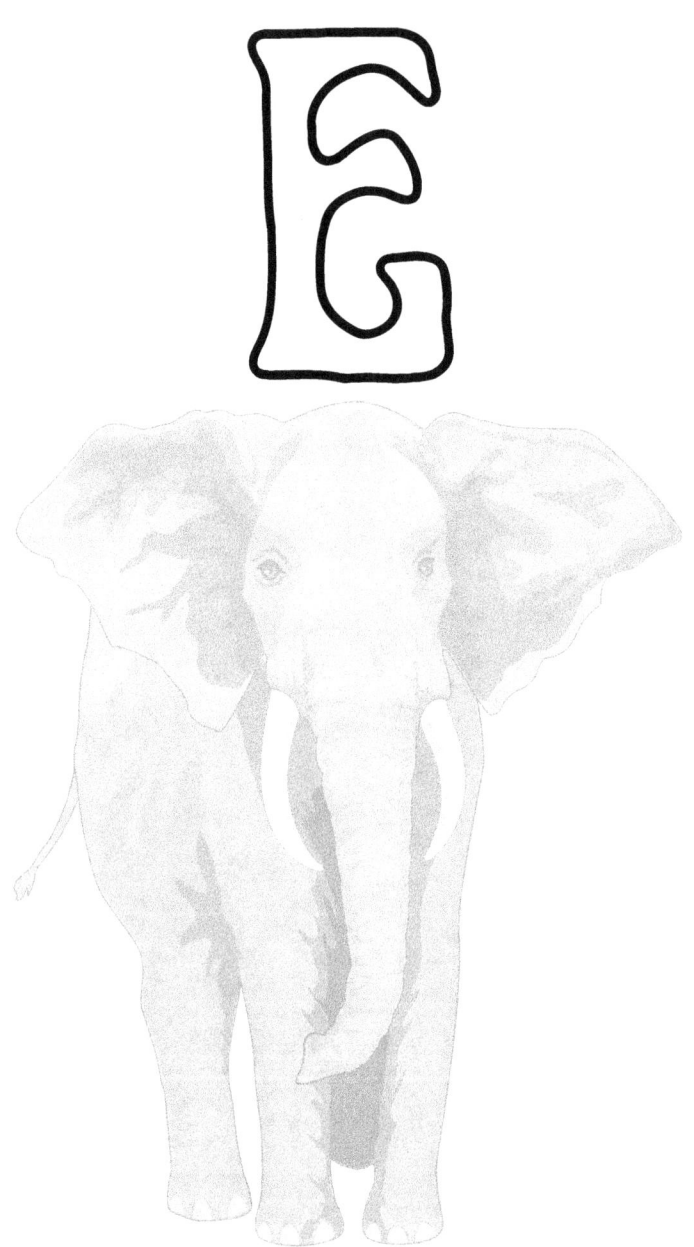

ELEPHANT

F

FISH

G

GOAT

H

HAT

I

ICE CREAM

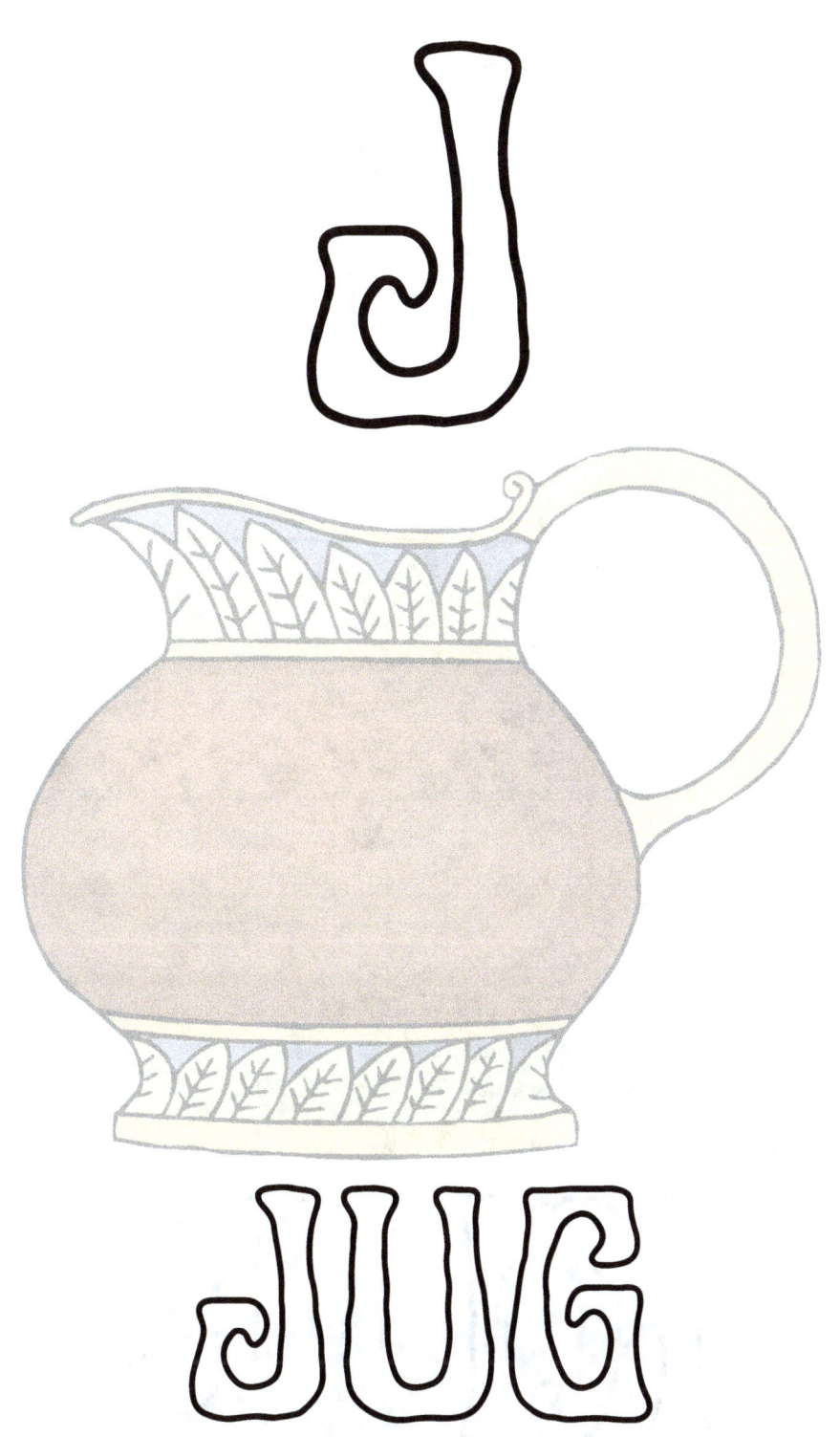

K

KITE

L

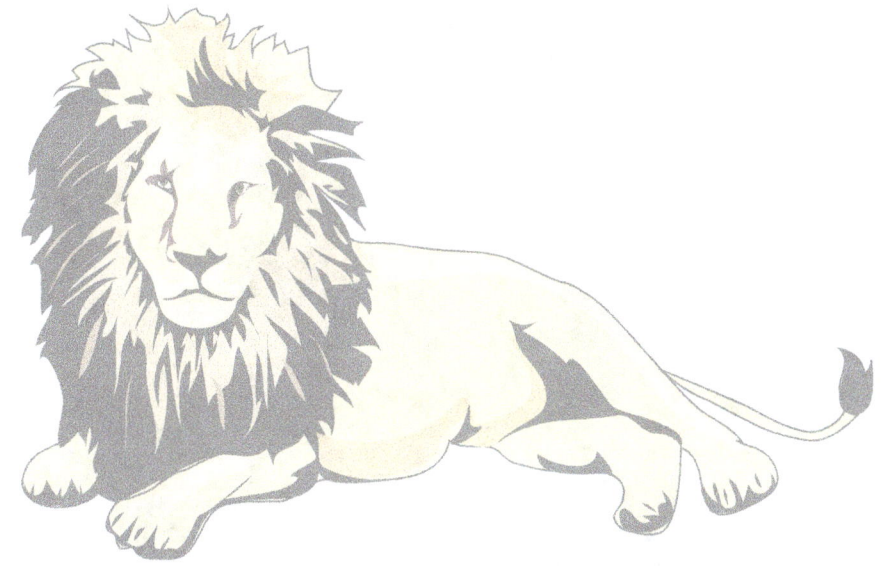

LION

M

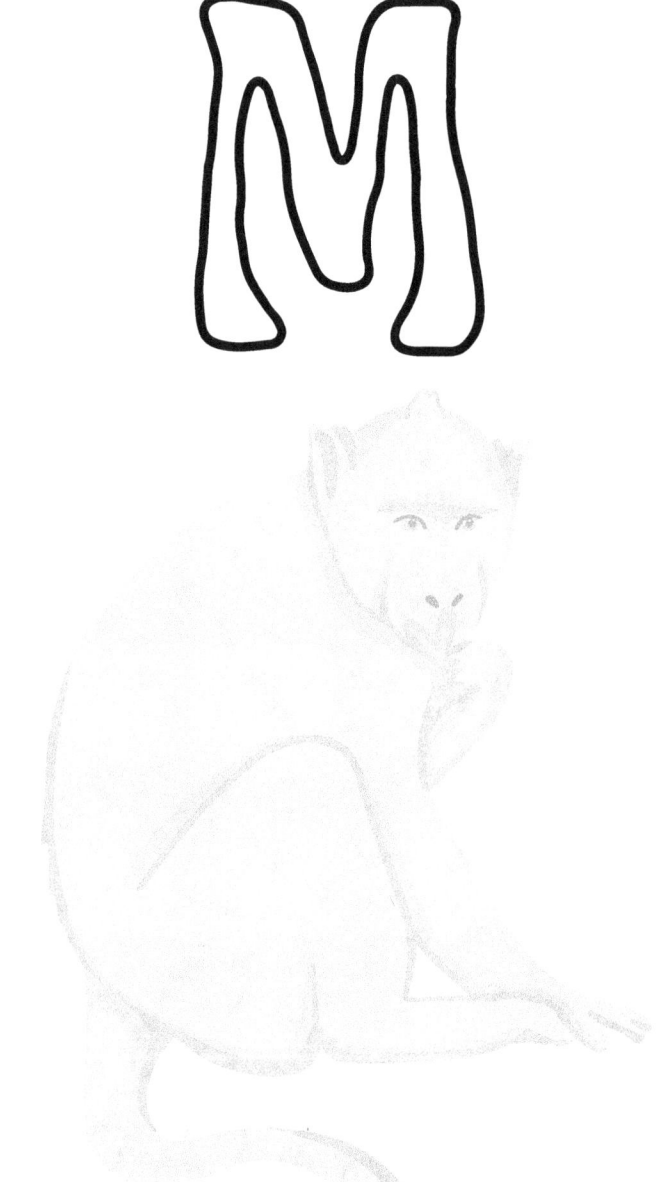

MONKEY

N

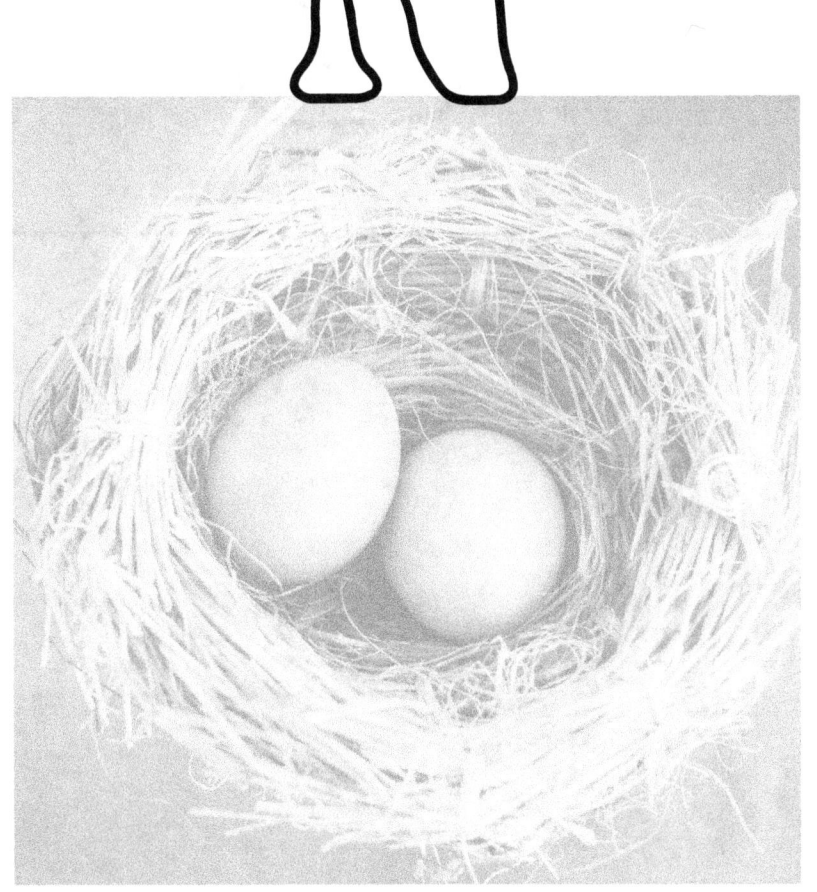

NEST

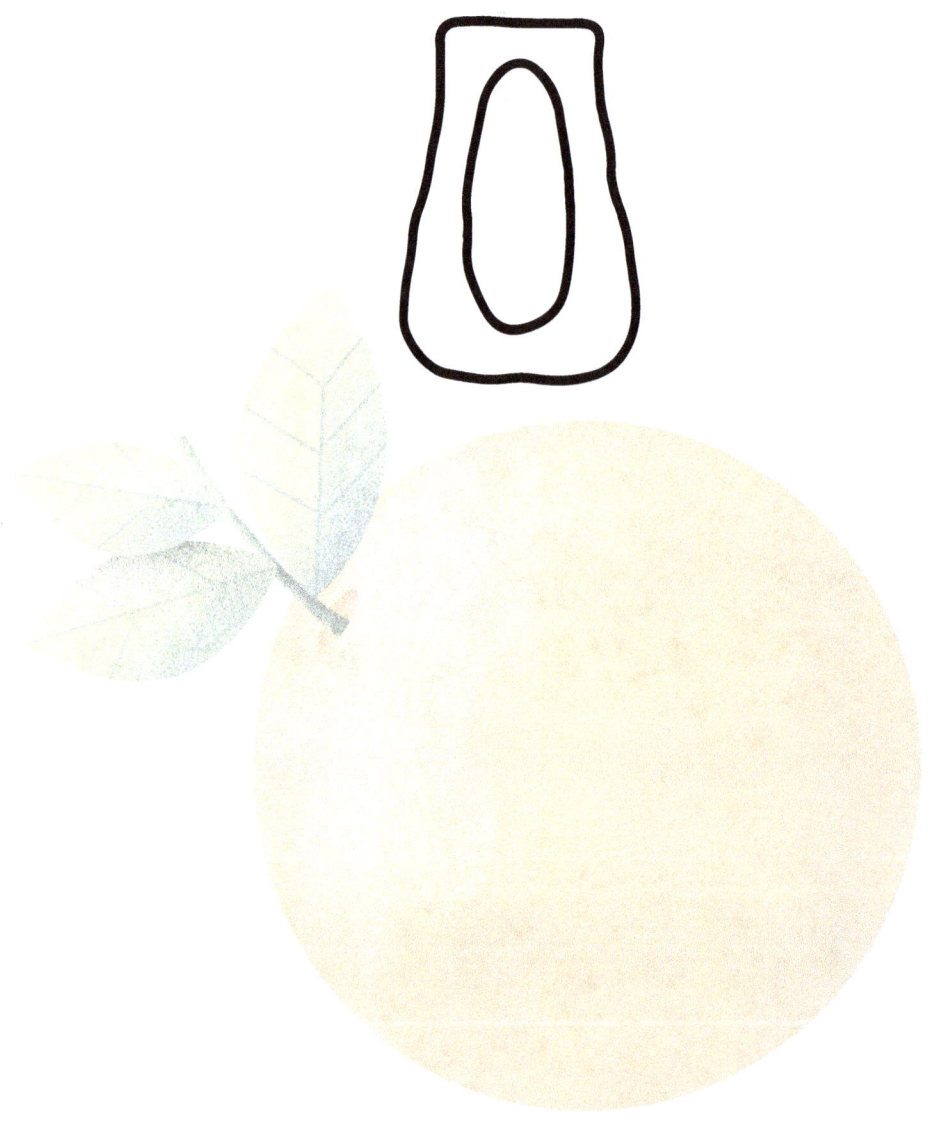

ORANGE

P

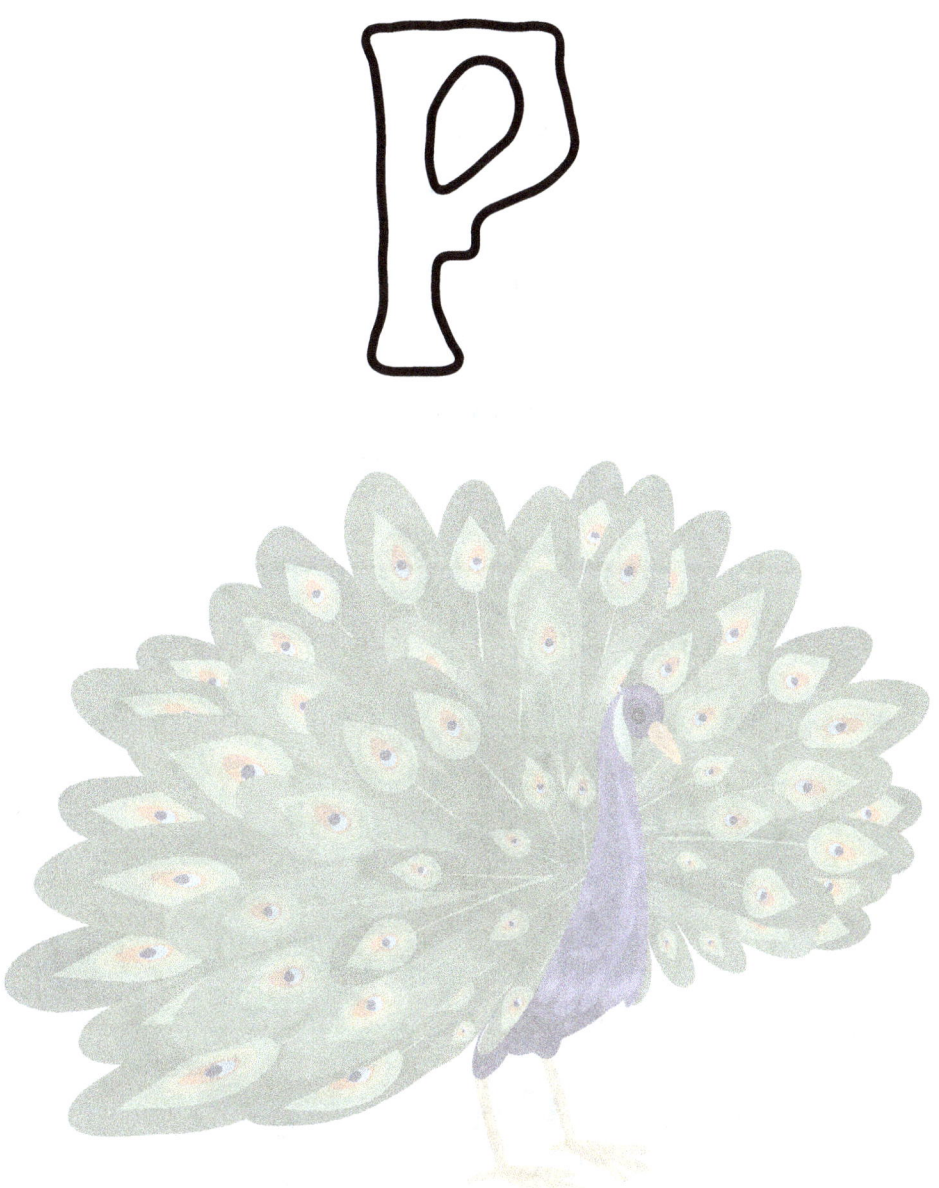

PEACOCK

Q

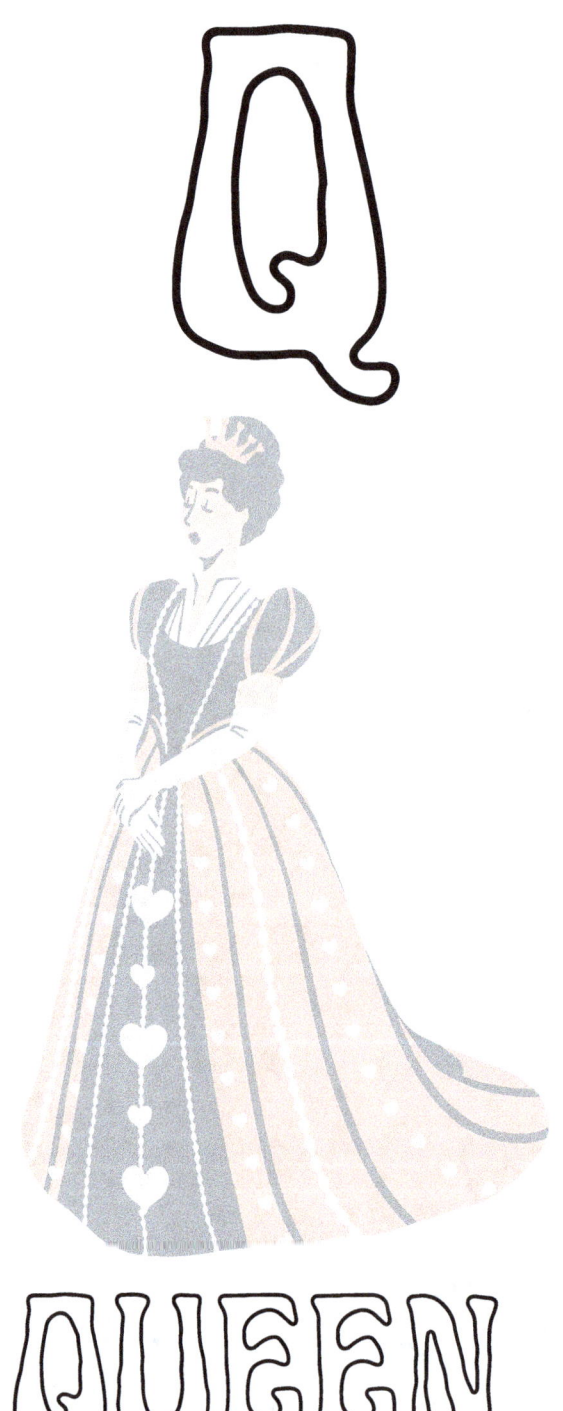

QUEEN

R

RABBIT

5

SHEEP

T

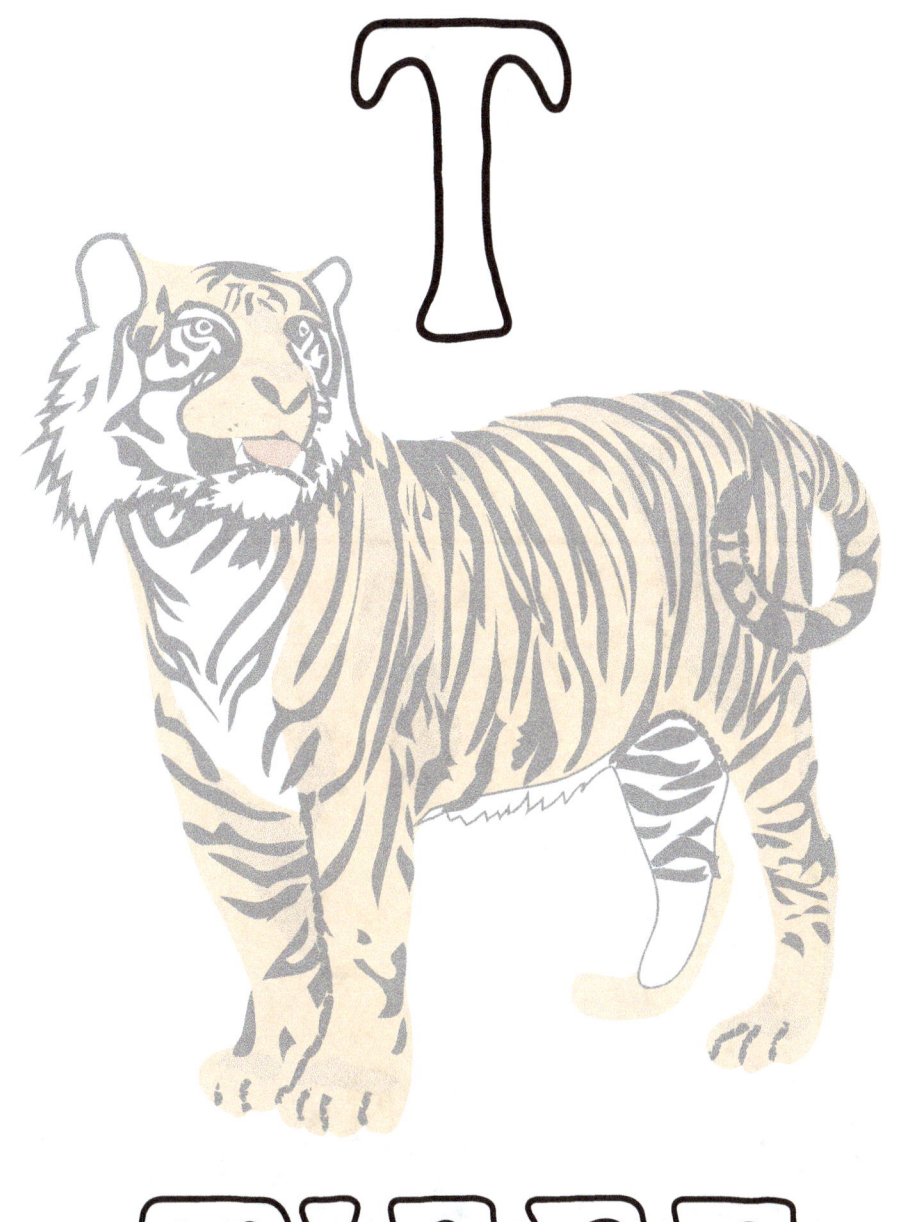

TIGER

U

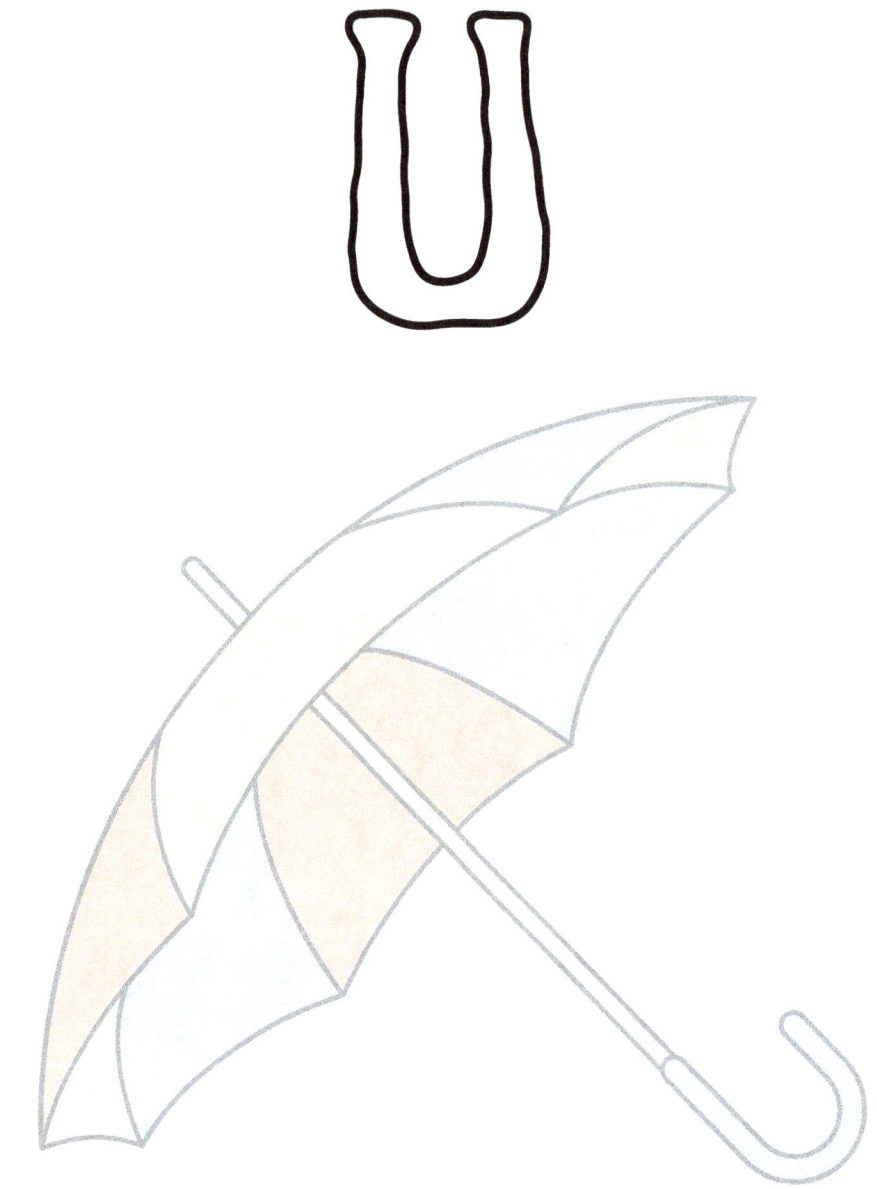

UMBERALA

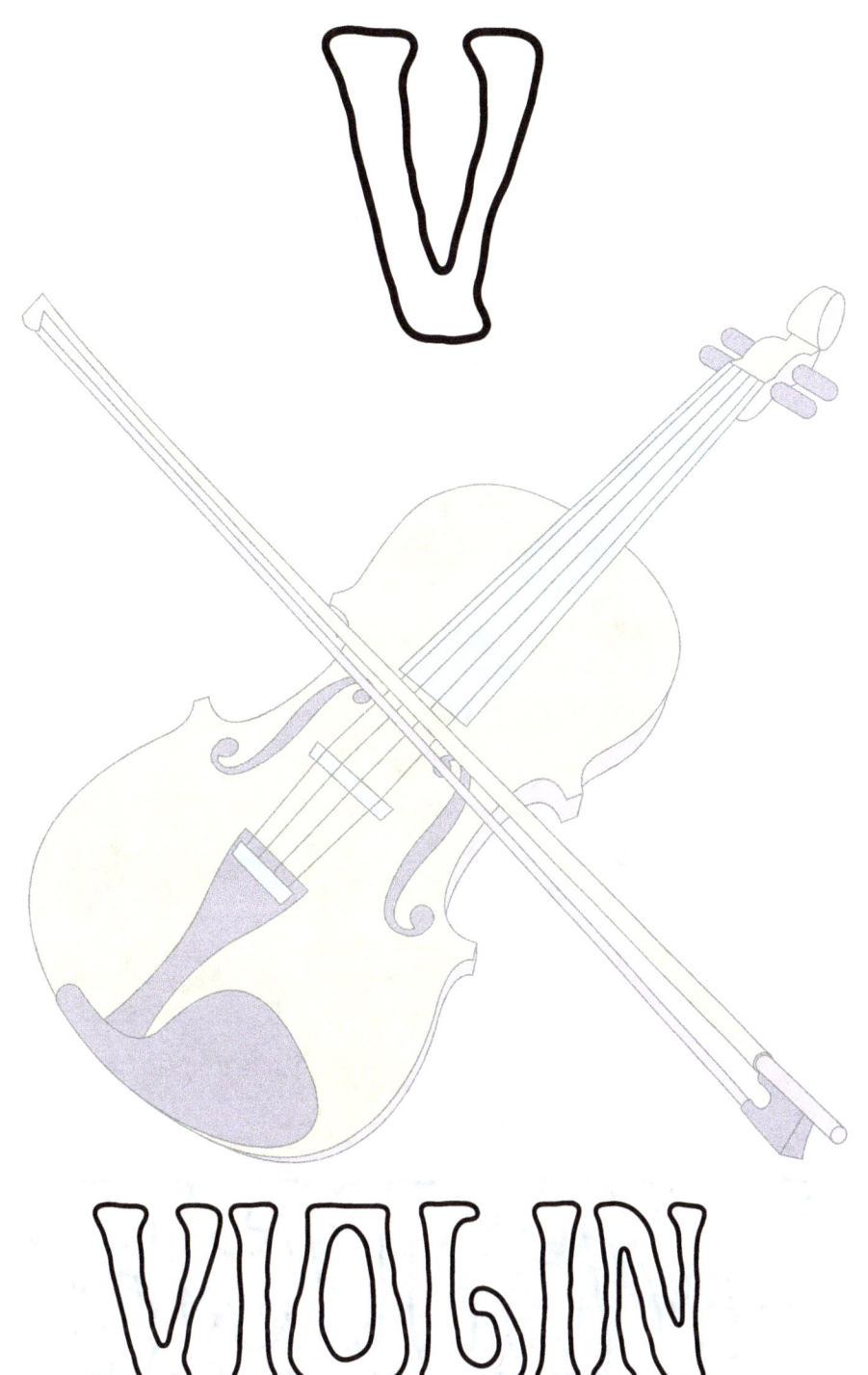

V

VIOLIN

W

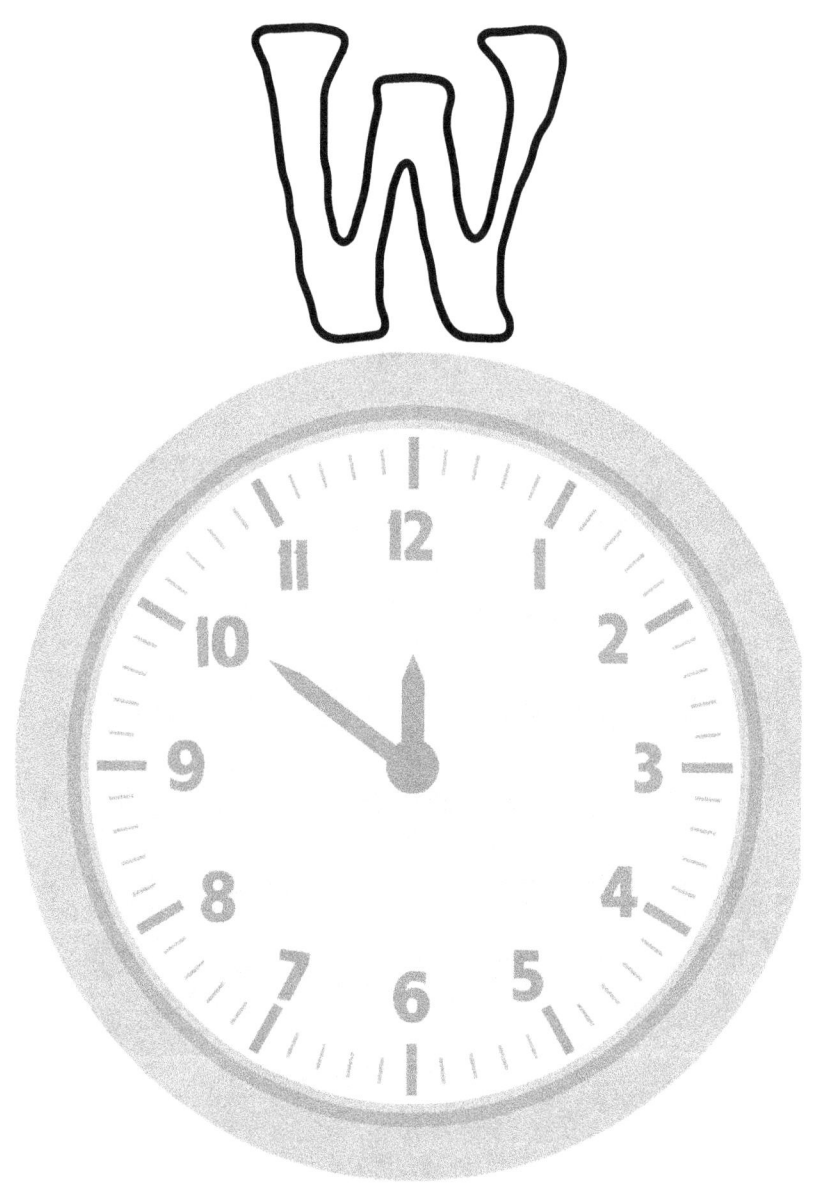

WATCH

X

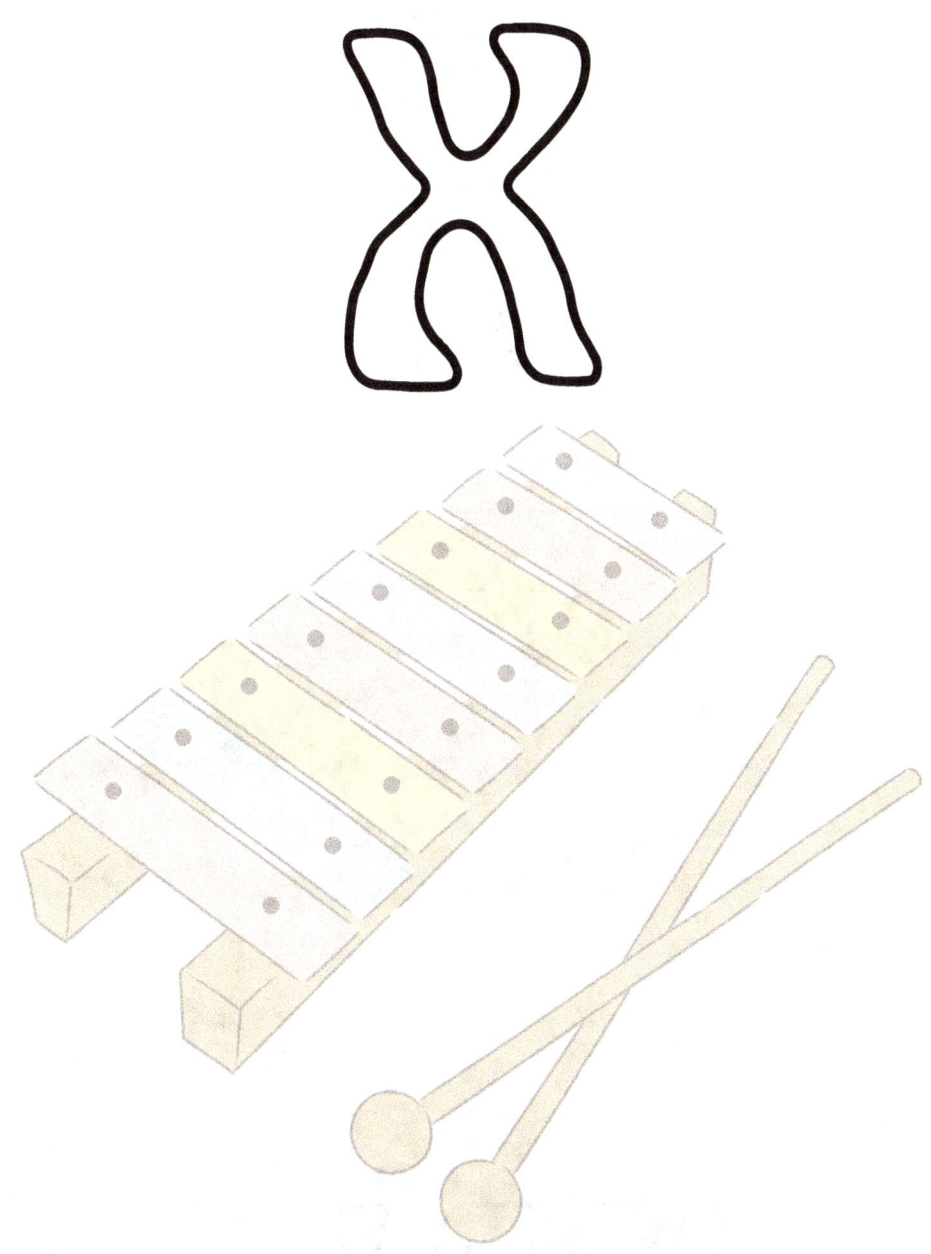

XYLOPHONE

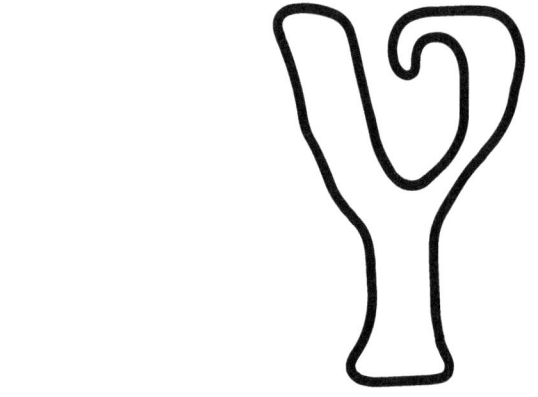

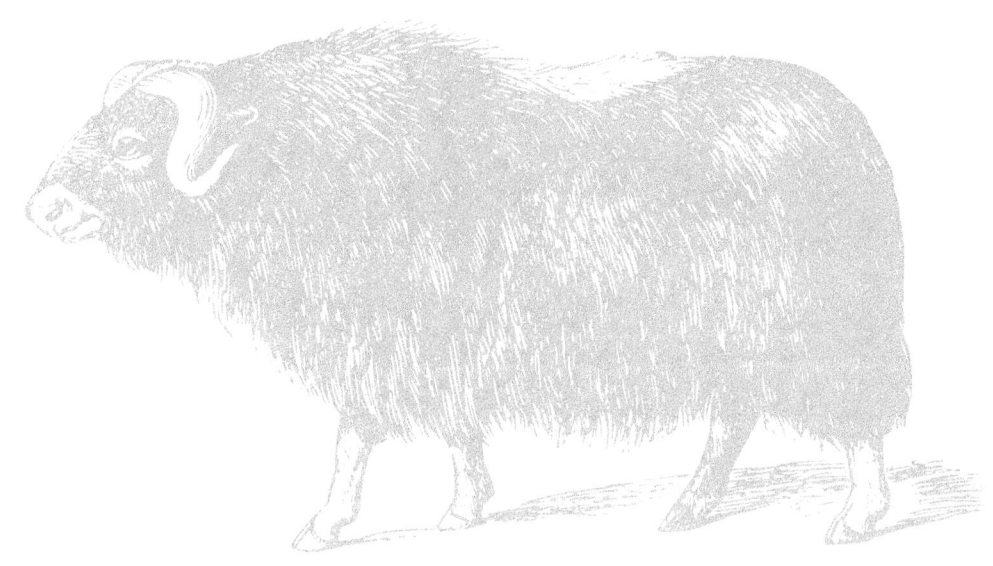

YAK

Z

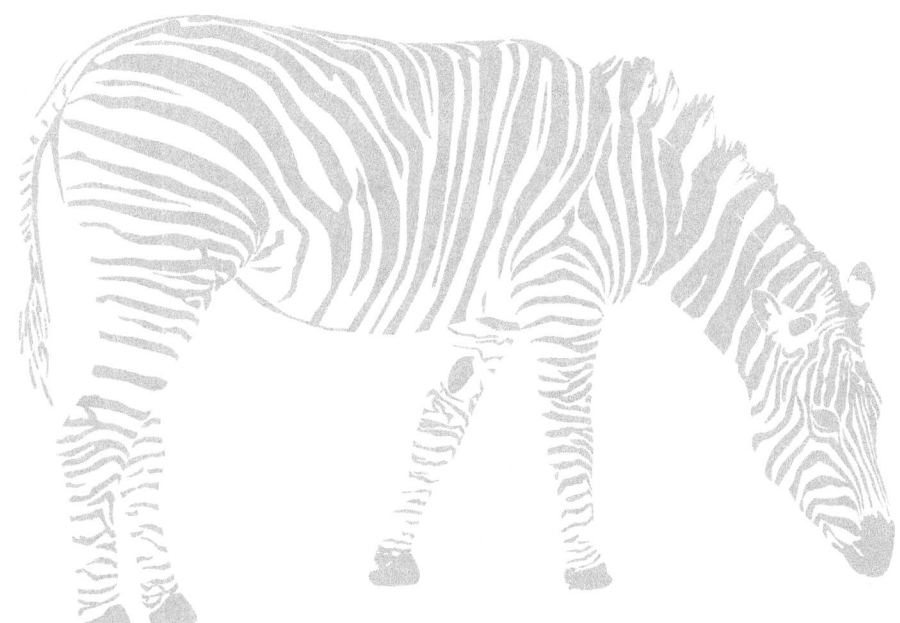

ZEBRA

www.ingramcontent.com/pod-product-compliance
Lightning Source LLC
Chambersburg PA
CBHW080914220526
45467CB00025BA/3172